Joachim Andersen

24 ETUDES, op.15

for Flute

Edited and with Practicing Suggestions by Louis Moyse

Preface by Marcel Moyse

ISBN 978-0-7935-5266-5

G. SCHIRMER, Inc.

DISTRIBUTED BY

HAL•LEONARD®
CORPORATION

7777 W. BLUEMOUND RD. P.O. BOX 13819 MILWAUKEE, WI 53213

Preface

In the teaching programs of all the European conservatories, the works of Joachim Andersen are given a place of honor. My first teacher, Adolphe Hennebains, successor to Paul Taffanel at the Paris Conservatory, always spoke of Andersen with enthusiasm and admiration. He liked to repeat again and again a sentence familiar to present day flutists: "Certainly the pianists are blessed by the etudes of Chopin, but we, the flutists, have the unique privilege to possess the etudes of Joachim Andersen."

It is very important to study these etudes employing a free interpretation of rhythms and articulation. By varying the rhythms one learns to know the different aspects of each etude. Changing the articulation frequently means to bring out the beauties of the melodic line in a most appealing manner. This not only increases the possibilities of mastering the difficulties inherent in each etude, it also is an ideal way to discover and understand the reason which lead to the composition of each etude.

This kind of study makes you reflect, helps you to understand and to progressively enfold the musical wealth that each etude contains. All this is important for any etude, but it is particularly important for the etudes of Joachim Andersen, for they are so beautiful and of such high musical quality.

To bring out the particular characteristic of each rhythm, to execute the articulations expressively with spirit, suppleness and elegance means to develop progressively for oneself the qualities of the interpretation, and to become aware of the fact that the music is definitely something more than just a perfect execution of a more or less rapid succession of notes. The French school has been so often spoken of that I would not benefit by the occasion offered me here to clearly re-affirm my opinion that the reason that the flute school of the Paris Conservatory has acquired such a great reputation is that it has been entrusted to artists of an extraordinary quality. I permit myself to be so affirmative about this because I remember Paul Taffanel telling us that all the traditions came to him from his master, Dorus, who himself was a pupil of Tulou. I had the unique opportunity to study the Andersen 'Opus 15' at the Paris Conservatory under the direction of Paul Taffanel. When they were played by him, each etude became a masterpiece of beauty and musicianship. What intelligence, clarity and technical simplicity helped underline for us the musical riches of each one of them.

I will never forget the reaction of Joachim Andersen when he was present at a performance of the well-known 'Third Etude in G Major' at the Paris Conservatory: "I never knew that I have written such a beautiful etude." With this phrase I would like to bring this little preface to an end and I hope that all flutists will share in the joys and the advantages which these etudes have brought me.

MARCEL MOYSE

Foreword

In practicing the following variants, one should keep in mind that they are not only designed to achieve a better performance of each etude but will also help the player to develop a better and stronger technique and thus master the general difficulties of his instrument.

All kinds of technical problems are dealt with in these exercises: fingering, slurs, articulation, tone, tonguing, suppleness of the lips, etc.

The method of practicing presented here can later on be applied to particular difficult passages in other music for the flute — etudes, solo pieces, sonatas, concertos,etc. — and will help the player to overcome them.

L.M.

Practicing suggestions by Louis Moyse

1.

To be practiced in the following variations:

2.

To be practiced *p dolce*; try to achieve an effortless, supple tone with maximum freedom of the lips.

Bars of even slurred 16ths (2, 4 etc.) may be varied in rhythm:

3.

First note and practice separately the melodic line:

When performing as written, try to bring out the melodic line.

4a

4b

7.

8.

1) is excellent practice for mixed tonguing — double tongue groups of 6 notes divided into 3, triple tongue groups of 6 divided into 2.

etc. legato sempre

9a

9b

16.

17.

This study is excellent for the study of various forms of *staccato*.

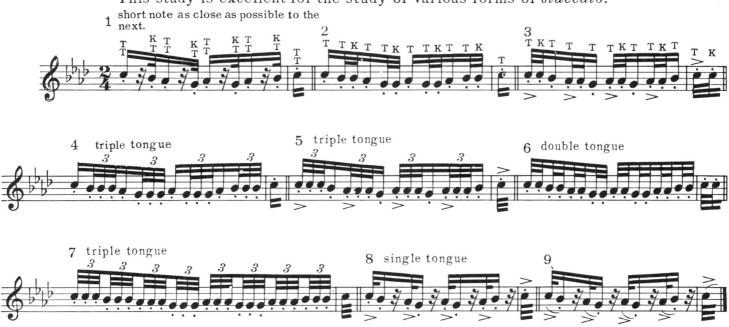

18

Rhythm and articulation variations to be applied to the middle section only:

Note that the middle section is constructed in four-bar phrases, the first measure being an "upbeat" to the more heavily accented second measure:

19

22

24

Variations apply to second section (Allegro con gravitá) and last section in D major (Meno Allegro)

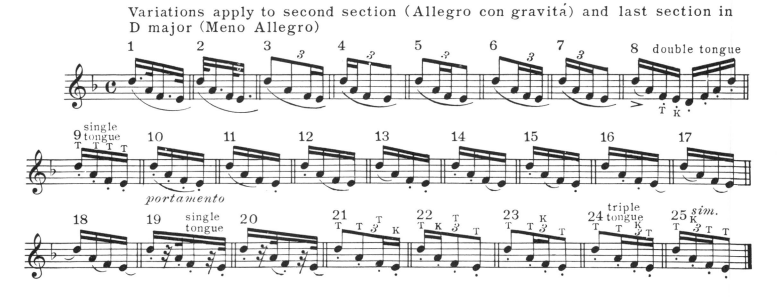

24 ETUDES

Joachim Andersen, Op. 15

Edited by LOUIS MOYSE

46633

24 ETUDES

Edited by LOUIS MOYSE

Joachim Andersen, Op. 15

1.

Allegro moderato M.M. ♩ = 112.

16

2.

Moderato M. M. ♩=100.

f con grandezza

18

3.

Allegro con brio M.M. ♩ = 69.

46633

4a.

4b.

5.

Allegro animato M. M. ♩ = 120.

f con alterezza

marc.

dim.

cresc. — *f* — *f*

marc.

p — *cresc.* —

f

6.

7.

8.

Andante M.M. ♩ = 84.

✱ repeat ad lib.

9a.

Allegretto giocoso M.M. ♩ = 92.
with single tongue

9b.

Allegretto giocoso M.M. ♩ = 92.
with double tongue

10.

11.

12.

13.

Allegro con fuoco M.M. ♩ = 132.

f *con disperatione*

14.

46633

15.

16.

17.

Moderato M. M. ♩ = 84.

18.

19.

20.

21.

46633

22.

23.

Moderato con vivezza M.M. ♩ = 76.

24.